GREAT MINDS® WIT & WISDOM

Grade 6 Module 4:
Courage in Crisis

Student Edition

COPYRIGHT STATEMENT

Published by Great Minds®.

ISBN: 978-1-68386-044-0

Table of Contents

Handout 2A: Glossary

Handout 2B: Optional Fluency Practice 1

Handout 3A: Art Vocabulary

Handout 3B: Boxes and Bullets Organizer–Chapter 2

Handout 4A: End-of-Module Task Process Chart

Handout 4B: Martin Luther King, Jr. Exemplar

Handout 4C: Topic Choice

Handout 4D: Chapter Note-Taking

Handout 4E: Frayer Model

Handout 5A: Source Credibility

Handout 6A: Pronoun Use

Handout 8A: Optional Fluency Practice 2

Handout 9A: Responses to Key Events

Handout 9B: –*ous* Suffix

Handout 10A: Note-Taking Organizer for Armstrong Text

Handout 11A: Main Idea and Supporting Details

Handout 12A: Note-Taking Organizer

Handout 13A: Excerpts About Shackleton

Handout 13B: Ernest Shackleton Exemplar

Handout 13C: Speaking and Listening Checklist

Handout 14A: Optional Fluency Practice 3

Handout 15A: Structure of *I Am Malala*

Handout 16A: Comparisons

Handout 17A: Events Organizer

Handout 17B: Consistent Style and Tone

Handout 19A: Event Analysis

Handout 19B: Optional Fluency Practice 4

Handout 19C: Style and Tone Revision

Handout 20A: Challenges and Responses

Handout 20B: Essay Graphic Organizer

Handout 21A: Central Ideas

Handout 21B: –*ive*, –*tive*, –*ative* Suffixes

Handout 22A: Optional Focusing Question Task 3 Graphic Organizer

Handout 23A: Source Integration
Handout 23B: Word Choice Analysis
Handout 24A: Event Organizer
Handout 24B: Effective Evidence Integration
Handout 24C: Frayer Model
Handout 25A: Word Choice Analysis
Handout 26A: Central Ideas
Handout 26B: Malala Yousafzai Exemplar
Handout 26C: Four Square Organizer
Handout 27A: Optional Informative/Explanatory Essay Graphic Organizer
Handout 28A: Claims and Reasoning
Handout 28B: "Malala Yousafzai–Nobel Lecture"
Handout 29A: Peer Content Review
Handout 29B: Peer Style and Conventions Edit
Handout 30A: "The Golden Hoard: An Ancient Afghan Treasure Is Recovered"
Handout 30B: Informative/Explanatory Writing Checklist
Handout 30C: Informative/Explanatory Writing Rubric
Volume of Reading Reflection Questions
Wit & Wisdom Parent Tip Sheet

Name

Date Class

Handout 2A: Glossary

Directions: This reference explains some words about navigation, exploration, and the Antarctic environment that you will encounter in *Shipwreck at the Bottom of the World*. Keep this handout in your Vocabulary Journal and refer to it as needed to support your learning, and record additional words as directed throughout the module.

Chapter	Word	Meaning
2	**latitude** (n.)	The distance between the equator and an area north or south on the earth's surface, usually measured in degrees.
	mast (n.)	The main support that rises from the keel (or the middle, bottom of the boat) and gives stability to a ship.
	hull (n.)	The frame of a ship.
	sledging (v.)	The act of riding in a sled.
	rations (n.)	A certain amount of something, such as food.
	scurvy (n.)	A disease that attacks the body due to a lack of vitamin C.
3	**steward** (n.)	Someone who is in charge of managing the stores or goods of a ship.
	squall (n.)	A violent gust of wind, indicative of a tumultuous storm.
	growlers (n.)	Large chunks of ice.
	iceberg (n.)	Large chunks of ice detached from glaciers that float in the sea.
4	**albatross** (n.)	A bird of legend that seamen fear and respect.
	leads (n.)	Open pathways not blocked by ice that boats can use.
	bridge (n.)	An elevated space above the rail on a ship.
	helm (n.)	The wheel by which a boat is operated.
	ice floe (n.)	A large expanse of floating ice.
5	**fo'c'sle hands** (n.)	Common sailors without rank.
	rigging (n.)	The ropes of a ship that are used to control the sails and manage the masts.
	meteorological (adj.)	Pertaining to meteorology and the study of the atmosphere and weather.
	astronomical (adj.)	Pertaining to astronomy and the study and observation of celestial bodies.

Chapter	Word	Meaning
6	**hummock** (n.)	A hill or ridge in an ice field.
	stern (n.)	The back part of a ship or boat.
	keel (n.)	Some type of enforcement situated in the middle, bottom part of a boat that extends lengthwise from stem to stern and aids in stability.
8	**galley** (n.)	A ship's kitchen.
	sextant (n.)	An astronomical instrument used to measure latitude and longitude and help determine one's position on earth.
11	**longitude** (n.)	the distance on the earth's surface east or west of the prime meridian at Greenwich, England, usually measured in degrees.
12	**riptide** (n.)	A tide which runs in the opposite direction of another tide and causes disturbance.
13	**foundering** (v.)	To fill with water and sink.
	tether (n.)	A rope or chain to secure or fasten objects together.
15	**ballast** (n.)	Something heavy carried by a boat to aid in stability.
16	**tacking** (v.)	To change the course of a ship and face it into the wind using a zigzag technique.
18	**crevasse** (n.)	An opening or fissure in a glacier.
19	**frostbite** (n.)	Injured tissue caused by extreme cold, which can result in gangrene.
	gangrene (n.)	The dying of tissue caused by a lack of circulation.

Name

Date Class

Handout 2B: Optional Fluency Practice 1

Directions:

1. Day 1: Read the text carefully and annotate to help you read fluently.
2. Each day:
   a. Practice reading the text aloud three to five times.
   b. Evaluate your progress by placing a checkmark in the appropriate, unshaded box.
   c. Ask someone (adult or peer) to listen and evaluate you as well.
3. Last day: answer the self-reflection questions at the end.

Just imagine yourself in the most hostile place on earth. It's not the Sahara or the Gobi Desert. It's not the Arctic. The most hostile place on earth is the Antarctic, the location of the South Pole. North Pole, South Pole–what's the difference? The Arctic is mostly water–with ice on top, of course–and that ice is never more than a few feet thick. But under the South Pole lies a continent that supports glaciers up to two miles in depth. Almost the entire southern continent is covered by ice. This mammoth icecap presses down so heavily that it actually distorts the shape of the earth. The ice never melts; it clings to the bottom of the world, spawning winds, storms, and weather that affect the whole planet.

And of all the weather it creates, the weather the Antarctic creates for itself is by far the worst. In the winter, the temperature can sink to 100 degrees below zero Fahrenheit. Cold air masses sliding down the sides of the glaciers speed up until they become winds of close to 200 miles per hour. When winter descends on the southern continent, the seas surrounding the land begin to freeze at the terrifying rate of two square miles every minute, until the frozen sea reaches an area of 7 million square miles, about twice the size of the United States. It is truly the most hostile environment this side of the moon. Just imagine yourself stranded in such a place.

In 1915, a British crew of twenty-eight men *was* stranded there, with no ship and no way to contact the outside world. They all survived.

Armstrong, Jennifer. *Shipwreck at the Bottom of the World: The Extraordinary True Story of Shackleton and the Endurance.* Knopf, 1998, p. 1.

Student Performance Checklist:	Day 1		Day 2		Day 3		Day 4	
	You	Listener*	You	Listener*	You	Listener*	You	Listener*
Accurately read the passage three to five times.								
Read with appropriate phrasing and pausing.								
Read with appropriate expression.								
Read articulately at a good pace and an audible volume.								

*Adult or peer

Self-reflection: What choices did you make when deciding how to read this passage, and why? What would you like to improve on or try differently next time? (*Thoughtfully answer these questions below.*)

Name

Date Class

Handout 3A: Art Vocabulary

Directions: This reference explains some art vocabulary that we will be using in this module to discuss the photographs in *Shipwreck at the Bottom of the World* as well as paintings. Keep this handout in your Vocabulary Journal and refer to it as needed to support your learning, and record additional words as directed throughout the module.

Word	Meaning
portrait (n.)	Painting or photograph of a person.
pose (n.)	How the subject of a portrait is sitting or standing, or what he or she is doing.
layout (n.)	How images and text are arranged on the page.
mood (n.)	The emotion or feeling that is evoked in the reader or viewer.
foreground (n.)	The area in a painting or photograph that seems closest to the viewer.
background (n.)	The area in a painting or photograph that seems the farthest away from the viewer.
composition (n)	How an artist organizes shapes, colors or values, and other components in a work of art.
texture (n.)	How the surface of an object looks like it would feel to the touch.
scale (n.)	The size of an object in relation to another object.
value (n.)	How light or dark a color looks.

Name

Date Class

Handout 3B: Boxes and Bullets Organizer–Chapter 2

Directions: Add key supporting details for each main idea in the Boxes and Bullets Organizer. Do not write the summary until instructed to do so.

Text: Chapter 2, *Shipwreck at the Bottom of the World*
Main Idea 1: Antarctica is a compelling and unique spot on earth.
Details: ▪ ▪ ▪ ▪
Main Idea 2: Many men from around the world have been inspired by Antarctica to undertake expeditions there.
Details: ▪ ▪ ▪ ▪
Main Idea 3: Shackleton was always pulled toward adventure, but exploration of Antarctica became his true calling.
Details: ▪ ▪ ▪ ▪

Main Idea 4: Shackleton did an excellent job financing and preparing for his expedition to cross Antarctica.
Details: ▪ ▪ ▪ ▪
Summary of chapter 2:

Name

Date Class

Handout 4A: End-of-Module Task Process Chart

EOM Task Process Chart			
Step Number	**Step Description**	**Resources**	**√ When Complete**
1	GET CLEAR ▪ Understand the EOM Task. ▪ Examine exemplar.	▪ Assessment 4A: End-of-Module Task. ▪ Handout 4B: Martin Luther King, Jr. Exemplar.	
2	CHOOSE PERSON	▪ Handout 4C: Topic Choice.	
3	FIND AND ASSESS SOURCES	▪ Handout 5A: Source Credibility.	
4	TAKE NOTES	▪ Handout 12A: Notes Graphic Organizer.	
5	PLAN ▪ Deconstruct exemplar. ▪ Review your notes. ▪ Sketch out the content you'll include. ▪ Plan how you'll use headings to organize your information. ▪ Confer with your peers and teacher as needed.	▪ All of the above. ▪ Handout 13B: Ernest Shackleton Exemplar. ▪ Handout 20B: Essay Graphic Organizer.	
6	DRAFT ▪ Draft your essay. ▪ Confer with your peers and teacher as needed.	▪ All of the above. ▪ Handout 26B: Malala Yousafzai Exemplar.	
7	REVIEW ▪ Complete Peer Review. ▪ Complete Peer Edit.	▪ Handout 29A: Peer Content Review. ▪ Handout 29B: Peer Style and Conventions Edit.	
8	REVISE ▪ Review and discuss feedback. ▪ Consult with your peers and teacher as needed. ▪ Revise the structure, content, and language of your essay.	▪ All of the above.	
9	SELF-ASSESS ▪ Complete Checklist. ▪ Review Rubric. ▪ Make final revisions.	▪ Handout 30B: Explanatory Writing Checklist. ▪ Handout 30C: Explanatory Writing Rubric.	
10	SUBMIT ▪ Submit your essay. ▪ You're done! ☺		

Name ______________________________

Date ______________ Class ______________

Handout 4B: Martin Luther King, Jr. Exemplar

Directions: Use the following exemplar essay as directed and to support your success on the End-of-Module Task.

The Courage of Martin Luther King, Jr.

Imagine a time when the color of your skin determined where you sat in a restaurant. Or if you could even enter a place of business. Or whether it was even safe for you to be in certain places. For African Americans in the 1950s, this was the hostile reality. Dr. Martin Luther King, Jr. personally experienced this unfair treatment, and in response, he dedicated his life to ending segregation. In response to the hostile environment of legal segregation and lack of rights for African Americans, Martin Luther King, Jr. acted heroically. He acted on behalf of the African-American community by staging protests demanding civil rights, and he took great personal risks to do so. These actions positively changed the lives of millions.

Unequal Treatment

Dr. King lived in America during a time of great hostility for African Americans. Racial segregation was legal, and African Americans were treated as though they were inferior to whites. Schools and public places were segregated. According to National Humanities Center Fellow Steven F. Lawson, "local and state authorities never funded black education equally nor did African Americans have equal access to public accommodations." This created a hostile environment for African Americans because they didn't have the same opportunities or resources as whites. At this time, each state was allowed to make its own rules about voting. Some states used poll taxes and literacy tests to make it harder for some African Americans to vote ("Martin Luther King Jr."). Without equal access to voting, African Americans couldn't vote against the laws that treated them unfairly. Dr. King believed that if people worked together, they could change this situation.

Heroic Action

To create this change, Dr. King acted on behalf of others and took extraordinary risks to bring about progress. Helping his fellow man, he began organizing people to peacefully stand up for racial equality. He worked tirelessly for others and used sit-ins, boycotts, and protest marches to draw attention to the injustices of segregation ("Martin Luther King, Jr. – Biography"). He also put himself in danger by bringing attention to the unfair treatment of African Americans. For example, Dr. King's home was bombed and he was assaulted four times ("Martin Luther King Jr. – Biography"). Even when he was the victim of violence, Dr. King displayed heroic action by continuing to call on others to engage in peaceful activism. He did not let others intimidate him into silence, and he never used violence as a response. Because of these heroic actions, Dr. King helped build the Civil Rights Movement, bringing people together to make change without using fear or violence.

Lasting Impact

Dr. King's peaceful organizing had an important impact in changing minds and laws. People around the country learned about how unequal treatment was affecting the lives of African Americans because of Dr. King's activism. Because of this increase in awareness, more and more people began to reject racist laws. On August 28, 1963, Dr. King led more than 200,000 people to the Lincoln Memorial in the March on Washington. There, he gave his famous "I Have a Dream" speech. The march and Dr. King's speech influenced Congress' passage of the Civil Rights Act of 1964. This law made it illegal to segregate public areas and discriminate against African Americans ("Martin Luther King Jr."). Dr. King's leadership helped congressmen understand that the law needed to be changed to ensure equality for African Americans. Dr. King kept working to "ensure that blacks could not be denied the right to vote by discriminating practices" ("Martin Luther King Jr. – Biography"). He led the March for Voting Rights, a fifty-four-mile march from Selma to Montgomery, Alabama. In response, Congress passed the Voting Rights Act in 1965. Again, Dr. King's organizing helped pass laws giving more protection to African Americans. He showed that change could come in a hostile environment if people joined together to send a message to those in power.

Dr. Martin Luther King, Jr. took heroic action to improve the lives of African Americans. His peaceful activism gave hope to millions of people. His organizing made politicians understand the importance of equality and brought change to our laws. Dr. King is truly a symbol of what one person can do to change the world.

Works Cited

History.com Staff. "Martin Luther King Jr." *History.com*, A&E Television Networks, 2009, Web. Accessed 19 Nov. 2016.

Lawson, Steven. "Segregation." *National Humanities Center*, Web. Accessed 19 Nov. 2016.

"Martin Luther King Jr. -- Biography." *Nobelprize.org*, Nobel Media AB, 10 Dec. 1964, Web. Accessed 19 Nov. 2016.

Name

Date Class

Handout 4C: Topic Choice

Directions: You can choose one of the following people to research for the End-of-Module Task, or you can choose someone on your own. Complete the bottom of page two, and submit for approval of your choice. A great resource to help you find someone is the "Nobel Prizes and Laureates" page of the Nobel Prize website – **http://witeng.link/0558**.

Nelson Mandela	**Mother Theresa**	**Aung San Suu Kyi**	**Kailash Satyarthi**
A South African activist who spent years in prison before becoming his country's first black president, he is known for his role in ending South Africa's oppressive system of apartheid. Received Nobel Peace Prize in 1993.	A Catholic nun who worked as a missionary in the slums of India, she is known for her role in caring and advocating for the poor. Received Nobel Peace Prize in 1979.	An outspoken critic of the dictatorship in Myanmar, she is known for spending years under house arrest as she fought for her country's democracy, eventually becoming its de facto leader. Received Nobel Peace Prize in 1991.	An Indian children's rights activist, he is known for speaking out against child labor and for founding the Save the Childhood Movement, which has protected the rights of thousands of children worldwide. Received Nobel Peace Prize in 2014.
Elie Weisel	**Alice Paul**	**Jane Addams**	**Rigoberta Menchu Tum**
A powerful Jewish writer who as a child was imprisoned at a German concentration camp, he is known for raising awareness about the horrors of the Holocaust. Received Nobel Peace Prize in 1986.	An American suffragist and feminist, she is known for her work campaigning for women's issues, particularly her role in the passage of the Nineteenth Amendment of the United States Constitution that gave women the right to vote.	An early feminist, she is known for her tireless work on behalf of women, children, and the poor, fighting for suffrage and the protection of civil liberties. Received Nobel Peace Prize in 1931.	A Mayan activist in Guatemala in the late twentieth century, she is known for standing up against the brutal Guatemalan military and raising awareness about the Mayan genocide. Received Nobel Peace Prize in 1992.
Harriet Tubman	**Dalai Lama**	**Anne Frank**	**Oskar Schindler**
An escaped slave who became an abolitionist, she is known for her role in the Underground Railroad during the nineteenth century that helped African Americans secure their freedom.	A holy, Buddhist monk seen as the spiritual leader of Tibet (a country from which he is exiled), he is known for being a passionate defender of the Tibetan people's right to democracy, something they have been denied since China invaded their country in 1949.	A Jewish teenager growing up during World War II, she is known for writing a poignant, powerful diary describing what is was like to be a Jewish girl hiding during the Nazi occupation.	A successful businessman and industrialist during World War II, he is known for later becoming a fierce protector of his Jewish employees, saving over one thousand lives during the Holocaust.
Sitting Bull	**Crazy Horse**	**Ruby Bridges**	**Jackie Robinson**
A Native American chief and Lakota holy man, he is known for uniting the Sioux tribes in their fierce resistance against the policies and initiatives of the United States in the nineteenth century.	A Native American chief of Sioux descent, he is known for his resistance to the forced removal of his people from their homeland by the United States government during the nineteenth century.	An African American activist, she is known for being the first African American child who desegregated an all-white school in the 1960's and who endured threats to her and her family's safety.	A celebrated and accomplished athlete, he is known for his role in integrating American sports by becoming the first African American to play in Major League Baseball.

Eleanor Roosevelt	Misty Copeland	Stephen Hawking	Rosa Parks
An admired First Lady of the United States, she is known for her defense of universal human rights and for her role in pushing the United States to join the United Nations, an organization of which she later became a delegate and key leader.	An African American ballet dancer, she is known for her tremendous talent and for becoming the first African American selected as a principal dancer for American Ballet Theatre.	An English physicist who has battled a crippling neurological disease, he is known for his brilliant work in the cosmology field, particularly his theories about black holes.	A civil rights activist, she is known for her role in igniting the Civil Rights Movement of the 1960's when she refused to give up her seat on a bus to a white passenger.

Witold Pilecki	Mahatma Gandhi
A Polish soldier during World War II, he is known for founding a resistance group in German-occupied Poland and for reporting German atrocities committed in concentration camps.	An Indian civil rights leader of the twentieth century, he is known for his role in securing Indian independence from Great Britain and for his devotion to non-violence as the most effective form of political activism.

1. I will research ______________________________ for my EOM Task.

2. I chose this person because

____

____

____

____

____

____

____

____

Name

Date Class

Handout 4D: Chapter Note-Taking

Directions: As you read for homework, record notes for the following two categories. For these notes, include quotes from the text or cite details from the photographs and follow up with a brief explanation. Please reference the first row as a model example. Try to complete at least two rows for each assigned chapter.

Chapter	Depiction of Antarctica as a hostile environment	The men's response to their environment
5	A blizzard "[pounds] the ship with gale force winds," causing the ice to press in on the ship (39).	The men must hunker down in the *Endurance* and not leave the ship. The men read books and "[huddle] around the stove" (39). They accept that they must wait out the storm, and they do not give into fear. Shackleton voices doubts to Worsley about the fate of the *Endurance*, but he does not share these doubts with the men. He puts on a brave face.

Name

Date Class

Handout 4E: Frayer Model

Directions: Complete the Frayer model for the word *incessant*.

Definition:	**Characteristics:**
Word: *incessant*	
Examples:	**Non-Examples:**

Name

Date Class

Handout 5A: Source Credibility

Directions: For your chosen individual, 1) record his or her name, 2) brainstorm key words that can be used in an online search, 3) type them into a search engine, and then 4) select a source to evaluate. Use this checklist to assess the source's credibility. Finally, after tallying up points, indicate whether the source is or is not credible by checking one of the boxes at the bottom of this handout.

Individual:		
Key Words:		
URL: http://		
Circle the number in the column that is the best answer.	**Yes**	**No/Not Sure**
Positives		
The article has an author, or if there is no author, I can identify the group responsible for the content of the article (e.g., History Channel, PBS, etc.).	1	0
The site has a .gov or .edu suffix.	1	0
The site provides a phone number or mailing address that I could use for contacting the person or organization for more information.	1	0
The main purpose of the site is to provide facts and information.	1	0
The site has been updated in the last three to six months.	1	0
There are sources cited for the article.	1	0
The information found on this site fits with other information I have gathered about my topic.	1	0
The web site is easy to navigate; there are options to return to the homepage, there is a site page or index, and it is easy to search.	1	0
Total (Positive):		

Negatives		
The site is clearly biased toward a specific opinion or point of view. Its purpose is to change people's opinions.	1	0
The site contains a lot of misspelled words and/or broken links.	1	0
The main purpose of the site is to sell a product or service.	1	0
The site does not link to other websites.	1	0
Total (Negative):		
TOTAL (Subtract the negative from the positive):		

When finished, subtract the negative tally from the positive tally, and total the source's credibility points. If your source has,

7 or more points: This is probably a credible source.

4–6 points: This might be a good source, but may be best used as a supplemental source, not your main source.

3 or less points: This is probably not worth including as a source.

Credible _________ **Not Credible** _________

Name

Date Class

Handout 6A: Pronoun Use

Directions: For each given sentence, identify the pronoun and its antecedent(s), and then evaluate whether the pronoun use is vague or clear.

Sentence	Pronoun	Antecedent(s)	Vague or Clear?
1. "[Shackleton]...dropped the heavy Bible on the cigarette case and gold coins, showing the crew the route they must take" (Armstrong 52).			
2. "On the lead sled went Shackleton, Wordie, Hussey, and Hudson, looking for the best route among the pressure ridges and tumbled ice floes. They were equipped with shovels, picks, and axes" (Armstrong 53).			
3. Bringing up the rear was the remainder of the crew pulling the boats on sledge runners. They weighed in at more than a ton apiece (adapted from Armstrong 54).			
4. "He and Worsley were worried about damaging the boats as they knocked their way across the ice" (Armstrong 54).			
5. Shackleton told Green to start adding large chunks of blubber to the crew's food. It kept them from freezing (adapted from Armstrong 54).			

Name

Date Class

Handout 8A: Optional Fluency Practice 2

Directions:

1. Day 1: Read the text carefully and annotate to help you read fluently.
2. Each day:
    a. Practice reading the text aloud three to five times.
    b. Evaluate your progress by placing a checkmark in the appropriate, unshaded box.
    c. Ask someone (adult or peer) to listen and evaluate you as well.
3. Last day: Answer the self-reflection questions at the end.

On January 1, Orde-Lees was skiing near the edge of the floe when a twelve-foot-long, fanged leopard seal lunged up out of the water and began humping toward him at astonishing speed. With a terrified yell, Orde-Lees stumbled across the ice toward camp. Suddenly, the animal lunged back into the water. As Orde-Lees had reached the opposite side of the floe, the leopard seal burst up out of the water in front of him, jaws agape. Screaming, Orde-Lees turned his skis and headed back. His frantic cries brought Wild out of his tent with a rifle, and Wild immediately dropped to one knee, raised the weapon, and began firing–and cursing furiously at Orde-Lees. The leopard seal now rushed toward Wild, who shot again and again. The animal was only thirty feet away from Wild when it fell at last. The entire crew was breathless.

An attack by a leopard seal was not a great way to begin life in the new camp. Everyone knew they were in worse circumstances than they had been even at Ocean Camp. They had fewer provisions and less equipment with them. The ice was growing so soft they often had to crawl on their hands and knees through saltwater slush, while hungry beasts that looked upon them as a new variety of food cruised through the dark waters just below them.

Armstrong, Jennifer. *Shipwreck at the Bottom of the World: The Extraordinary True Story of Shackleton and the Endurance*. Knopf, 1998, p. 66.

Student Performance Checklist:	Day 1		Day 2		Day 3		Day 4	
	You	Listener*	You	Listener*	You	Listener*	You	Listener*
Accurately read the passage three to five times.								
Read with appropriate phrasing and pausing.								
Read with appropriate expression.								
Read articulately at a good pace and an audible volume.								

*Adult or peer

Self-reflection: What choices did you make when deciding how to read this passage, and why? What would you like to improve on or try differently next time? (*Thoughtfully answer these questions below.*)

Name

Date Class

Handout 9A: Responses to Key Events

Directions: Complete the table below for your small group's assigned key event, referencing the notes you completed for homework and making sure to cite textual evidence in your responses.

Chapter	Key Event	How does this key event...	
		...inspire heroism in the men's response?	...inspire heroism in Shackleton's response?
12	A riptide almost "[engulfs] the three puny bcats with a deluge of ice and slush" (79).		
	A crack opens up on a floe they are camped on, and a man falls into the icy water. (79–80)		
13	The men are caught like "rats in a trap" as the iceberg they are camped on begins to deteriorate. (83)		

13	Worsley checks their position and realizes that they are not making progress. (84–85)		
	The men experience another long night of no sleep and exposure to the bitter cold. (84–86)		
	The boats must separate from each other. Worsley goes on ahead in the *Dudley Docker*, while Shackleton stays tethered to the *Wills*. (77–78)		

Name

Date Class

Handout 9B: *-ous* Suffix

Directions: Complete the table. Use a dictionary for *anxiety* and *peril* before developing your own definition for *anxious* and *perilous*.

Noun	Meaning	Noun plus *-ous*	Meaning
danger		dangerous	
		disastrous	
		joyous	
anxiety		anxious	
peril		perilous	

Name

Date Class

Handout 10A: Note-Taking Organizer for Armstrong Text

Directions: This activity provides you with an opportunity to practice evidence-gathering for the End-of-Module (EOM) Task, using chapter 14. Review the chapter and collect relevant evidence for each of the sections of EOM Task using the tables below.

Hostile Environment	
Evidence and Page Number	**Explanation**
"The men ate, slept, and ate again, standing around in small groups, stupefied and silent" (90).	The passage to Elephant Island has drained the men to the point that they have no energy left for anything except eating and sleeping. They are exhausted and no longer show any of the exuberance they once felt after leaving the ice.

Heroic Actions		
	Evidence and Page Number	**Explanation**
The Crew	"Frank Wild and five men pushed the Wills out into the crashing surf and rowed off in search of a new landing site" (91).	This expedition takes nine hours to complete. The men are exhausted, but they know they must find a new spot to camp on Elephant Island if the group is to survive. They put aside their own needs (like resting) to help the entire group.

Name

Date Class

Heroic Actions		
	Evidence and Page Number	Explanation
Shackleton		

In the space below, write one or two sentences summarizing how the crew's and Shackleton's heroic actions in response to the hostile environment of Antarctica impact the group's overall well-being:

Name

Date Class

Handout 11A: Main Idea and Supporting Details

Directions: Complete the table below for your group's assigned factor(s).

Main Idea of Chapter 17: Many factors help the men endure the impossible.	
Factor	**Evidence and Explanation**
Shackleton's leadership	Worsley and Crean trust their leader. Shackleton makes a combination of wise and risky decisions on this last leg of the journey, and even when the men have doubts (like the moment when Shackleton tells them they need to slide down the mountain), they follow the Boss's orders. Because he makes good decisions, the men stick together and follow him with few questions.
Reliance upon faith	
Reliance upon hope	
Devotion to others	

Main Idea of chapter 17: Many factors help the men endure the impossible.	
Factor	**Evidence and Explanation**
Teamwork	
Making the best of things	

Name

Date Class

Handout 12A: Note-Taking Organizer

Directions: Complete the information and organizer below for each of your credible sources. Make sure to indicate whether you are directly quoting from your source or paraphrasing information as well as to cite the page number if using a print source.

Name of Individual	
Source Title	
Source Author	
Date	
Publisher or web link:	

Hostile Environment	
Evidence	**Elaboration**

Heroic Actions	
Evidence	**Elaboration**

Positive Impact	
Evidence	**Elaboration**

Name

Date Class

Handout 13A: Excerpts about Shackleton

Directions: Read and discuss the following quotations about Shackleton, using the provided glossary as needed.

"Shackleton is a hero of perfect ambivalence, a man filled with enough hubris to prompt him to take his men to meet almost certain disaster, but possessed of such extraordinary leadership skills to pull off a victory of mythological proportions in a story of man versus nature that ranks with the best tall tales." From Archer, Bert. "The Most Remote Museum on Earth." *Slate*, The Slate Group, Graham Holdings Company, 16 May 2014, Web. Accessed 6 Dec. 2016.	
"Shackleton is revered today for his leadership–not his hubris, never that–which is another powerful takeaway from this story. Competency, adaptability and decisiveness, with the appropriate respect and humbleness in the face of the enduring power of the sea–those are qualities we need as much today as did the iron men who stoically ventured through the age of polar exploration." From Sisson, William. "Century-Old Lessons From the 'Bottom of the World.'" *Soundings*, Cruz Bay Publishing, Active Interest Media, 29 Mar. 2013, Web. Accessed 6 Dec. 2016.	
What is similar about these two descriptions of Shackleton?	**What is different about these two descriptions of Shackleton?**

Glossary

Word	Meaning
ambivalence (n.)	Having conflictual feelings about someone or something.
hubris (n.)	Excessive pride; arrogance.
revered (v.)	Worshipped or honored.
competency (n.)	Properly and sufficiently qualified.
stoically (adv.)	Hiding emotion in reaction to something bad.

Name

Date Class

Handout 13B: Ernest Shackleton Exemplar

Directions: Use the following exemplar essay as directed and to support your success on the End-of-Module Task.

Shackleton's Bravery

Do you think you could survive in an environment with temperatures as low as 100 degrees below zero and winds blowing almost 200 miles per hour? In this type of hostile climate, it would be almost impossible to survive. Yet that is exactly what Earnest Shackleton and his crew of 27 did in the years of 1915–1916. After their ship, the *Endurance*, got stuck in the ice, it broke apart and sank. Shackleton had to help his crew survive and find a way to get them home again. In response to an incredibly hostile environment, Shackleton always acted for the good of others, and took extraordinary and risky steps to do so. These heroic actions resulted in every man making it home sane and alive.

A Hostile Environment

Antarctica is inhospitable to man. It is so cold in the winter that even the ocean freezes, at the amazing speed of "two square miles every minute" (Armstrong 1). For Shackleton and his men, this environment became even more hostile and frightening after their boat the *Endurance* twisted apart under the terrifying strength of the ice pressing up against it until it broke and then sank (Archer). Without the ship's protection, surviving in the Antarctica was even more challenging. Shackleton led his men in creating a camp on the ice floes where the men were always wet and frozen, and had only the lifeboats for shelter (Armstrong). It is hard to imagine a more hostile environment.

Heroic Action

Shackleton's response to being shipwrecked was to focus on the well-being of his crew and take extraordinary risks to ensure their survival. To help his men not panic, Shackleton made sure the men had a sense of order and purpose. For example, he set up daily routines for his men to follow that "[kept] the crew from going crazy with cabin fever" (31). He made a plan so that each crew member would know what they should do if an emergency arose. Shackleton knew that if there wasn't this structure, the men might get discouraged and worried. He also constantly checked on his men's morale and found ways to distract them. Besides lifting his men's morale, he took extraordinary, heroic actions to save the lives of his crew. According to the diary of crew member Thomas Orde-Lees, Shackleton saved one of his fellow crew members, Ernest Holness, when he fell into the icy sea after their ice floe cracked in half. Because of Shackleton's quick thinking, he managed to pull Holness out of the water, and he did not rest until every man was out of danger's way. Later again displaying heroic action, Shackleton volunteered to sail 800 miles across the ocean and to walk twenty-nine miles across South Georgia Island to find help for his crew. At one point, he slid down a mountain into unknown territory, risking possible death so that he could save his men's lives (Armstrong). Shackleton knew that reaching the whaling station on South Georgia Island was the only way his crew would survive, and he did whatever it took to get there. By placing his men's needs first, Shackleton demonstrated heroic action.

Powerful Impact

Shackleton's actions had an enormous impact. By focusing on his men's morale, he helped save the men's sanity when they were near breaking. By giving every man a purpose at camp, they didn't feel helpless. By making sure they had a routine, they stayed distracted and felt safe (Armstrong). They kept their heads and a sense of optimism because Shackleton kept them focused on making it through each day. Even more important, Shackleton's extraordinary actions and risk-taking resulted in every man surviving this ordeal. Because he took steps to keep his men safe and pushed himself to reach the whaling village at South Georgia Island, he was able to bring everyone home to England.

We sometimes use the word *heroic* lightly, but it is truly a word that describes Ernest Shackleton and his devotion to his crew in Antarctica. When circumstances seem overwhelmingly hostile, it can be humbling to see what heroic behavior people are capable of.

Works Cited

Archer, Bert. "The Most Remote Museum on Earth." *Slate*, The Slate Group, Graham Holdings Company, 16 May 2014, Web. Accessed 6 Dec. 2016.

Armstrong, Jennifer. *Shipwreck at the Bottom of the World: The Extraordinary True Story of Shackleton and the Endurance*. Knopf, 1998.

Orde-Lees, Thomas. "Night of 9th–10th 1916." PBS, Feb. 2002, Web. Accessed 27 Sept. 2016.

Name

Date Class

Handout 13C: Speaking and Listening Checklist

Directions: Evaluate your participation by marking + for "yes" and Δ for "needs improvement" in the appropriate boxes. Ask someone (adult or peer) to evaluate your participation as well.

	Self +/Δ	Peer +/Δ	Teacher +/Δ
I used text evidence to support my opinion.			
I asked questions.			
I responded to questions.			
I made relevant observations.			
I followed all the rules for speaking in a group.			
I set and met my participation goal.			
I acknowledged and elaborated on comments from my peers.			
I balanced my use of statements and questions.			
I listened for my peers' claims and reasons and responded to both.			
I evaluated and responded to my peers' claims and reasons.			
I stayed engaged in the conversation the whole time.			
I brought the conversation back on topic when needed.			
I used appropriate, formal, academic language. For example:			
I used vocabulary that I learned in this module, such as these words:			
Total number of +'s			

1. What is your goal for today's Socratic Seminar to improve your participation?

____

____

2. Did you meet your goal? Why or why not?

____

____

____

3. What will your goal be for the next discussion?

____

____

Name

Date Class

Handout 14A: Optional Fluency Practice 3

Directions:

1. Day 1: Read the text carefully and annotate to help you read fluently.
2. Each day:
   a. Practice reading the text aloud three to five times.
   b. Evaluate your progress by placing a checkmark in the appropriate, unshaded box.
   c. Ask someone (adult or peer) to listen and evaluate you as well.
3. Last day: Answer the self-reflection questions at the end.

Just after we passed the Little Giants snack factory and the bend in the road not more than three minutes from my house, the van slowed to a halt. It was oddly quiet outside.

"It's so calm today, " I said to Moniba. "Where are all the people?"

I don't remember anything after that, but here's the story that's been told to me:

Two young men in white robes stepped in front of our truck.

"Is this the Krushal School bus?" one of them asked.

The driver laughed. The name of the school was painted in black letters on the side.

The other young man jumped onto the tailboard and leaned in the back, where we were all sitting.

"Who is Malala?" he asked.

No one said a word, but a few girls pointed in my direction. He raised his arm and pointed at me. Some of the girls screamed and I squeezed Moniba's hand.

Who is Malala? I am Malala, and this is my story.

Yousafzai, Malala and Patricia McCormick. *I Am Malala: How One Girl Stood Up for Education and Changed the World.* Young Reader's Edition, Little, Brown and Company, 2014, pp. 6-7.

Student Performance Checklist:	Day 1		Day 2		Day 3		Day 4	
	You	Listener*	You	Listener*	You	Listener*	You	Listener*
Accurately read the passage three to five times.								
Read with appropriate phrasing and pausing.								
Read with appropriate expression.								
Read articulately at a good pace and an audible volume.								

*Adult or peer

Self-reflection: What choices did you make when deciding how to read this passage, and why? What would you like to improve on or try differently next time? (*Thoughtfully answer these questions below.*)

Name

Date Class

Handout 15A: Structure of *I Am Malala*

Directions: Complete the table for each chapter in part one as you read the text. After you complete all the chapters in part one, respond to the question in the last row. Repeat for parts two, three, four, and five of the text.

Part One: "Before the Taliban"			
Chapter Number	**Chapter Title**	**What happens in this chapter?**	**How does this chapter connect/relate to the ones before it?**
1	As Free As a Bird	It talks about Malala's family	
2	Dreams	It talks about the hard Life as a women	
3			
4			
5			
What main ideas are developed in part one?			

Part Two: "A Shadow Over Our Valley"			
#	Chapter Title	What happens in this chapter?	How does this chapter connect/relate to the ones before it?
6			
7			
8			
9			
10			
What main ideas are developed in part two?			

Name

Date Class

Part Three: "Finding My Voice"			
#	Chapter Title	What happens in this chapter?	How does this chapter connect/relate to the ones before it?
11			
12			
13			
14			
15			
16			
17			

18			
19			

What main ideas are developed in part three?

Part Four: "Targeted"			
#	**Chapter Title**	**What happens in this chapter?**	**How does this chapter connect/relate to the ones before it?**
20			
21			
22			
23			

Name

Date Class

What main ideas are developed in part four?

Part Five: "A New Life, Far from Home"			
#	Chapter Title	What happens in this chapter?	How does this chapter connect/relate to the ones before it?
24			
25			
26			
27			
28			
29			

30			
31			
32			
33			
34			
35			
36			

What main ideas are developed in part five?

Name

Date Class

Handout 16A: Comparisons

Directions: Reread and annotate the excerpt below, marking the comparisons Yousafzai and McCormick are making between the girls' lives outside of school (O) and what they experienced in school (I). Complete columns A and B with evidence from the text and complete column C. Answer the question below the table.

Because inside the Krushal School, we flew on wings of knowledge. In a country where women aren't allowed out in public without a man, we girls traveled far and wide inside the pages of our books. In a land where many women can't read the prices in the markets, we did multiplication. In a place where, as soon as we were teenagers, we'd have to cover our heads and hide ourselves from the boys who'd been our childhood playmates, we ran as free as the wind (Yousafzai and McCormick 34).

A	B	C
Life Outside of the School (O)	**Life Inside of the School (I)**	**What opportunity were the girls getting in school that they wouldn't have otherwise experienced?**
"In a country where women aren't allowed in public without a man" (34)	"We girls traveled far and wide inside the pages of our books" (34)	
	"We did multiplication" (34)	
"In a place where, as soon as we were teenagers, we'd have to cover ourselves from the boys who'd been our childhood playmates" (34)		

How are these ideas connected to a main idea in part 1 of the text?

Name

Date Class

Handout 17A: Events Organizer

Directions: Complete the chart for chapters 6 and 7, and answer the question following it.

Actions of Fazlullah and the Taliban	Reactions of those who believe Fazlullah's message	Reactions of Malala, her father, or others who oppose Fazlullah
1. Fazlullah claims that people should stop listening to music, going to the movies, and dancing or "God will send another earthquake to punish [them] all" (39).		
2. Fazlullah talked about "bringing back Islamic law" (40).		
3.	"Some took their TVs, DVDs, and CDs to the public square, where the Radio Mullah's men set them on fire" (46).	
4.		Malala's mother "insisted that [she] never walk to school by [herself]" (48).

Actions of Fazlullah and the Taliban	Reactions of those who believe Fazlullah's message	Reactions of Malala, her father, or others who oppose Fazlullah
5.	People followed Fazlullah's rules to keep from being flogged or killed.	

6. In three or fewer sentences, summarize how Fazlullah created a hostile environment in Mingora and Swat Valley.

Name

Date Class

Handout 17B: Consistent Style and Tone

Directions: Read the two passages, noting the consistency of style and tone. Answer the questions below the text.

A	B
The Taliban. As soon as I would hear that word, my ears would perk up. I'd think back to the talk I'd had with my father when we were in Shangla. The Taliban seemed like something far away then. Like something bad in a distant place. Even many of my father's friends believed that despite how popular Fazlullah was becoming and his association with the Taliban in Pakistan, they were still too far away to be a concern, but my father warned them that there would come a day when the Taliban would reach our valley. (Adapted from Yousafzai and McCormick 42.)	As soon as I heard the word *Taliban*, my interest would be piqued and I would consider the conversation that I had with my father when we were in Shangla. At that time, the Taliban seemed like a terrible force that was at a considerable distance, and therefore of no immediate concern. Even many of my father's friends believed that despite how popular Fazlullah was becoming and his association with the Taliban in Pakistan, they were still too far away to be a concern, but my father warned them that there would come a day when the Taliban would reach our valley. (Adapted from Yousafzai and McCormick 42.)

How do the style and/or tone of Passage A impact its meaning?

How do the style and/or tone of Passage B impact its meaning?

Name

Date Class

Handout 19A: Event Analysis

Directions: Reread the text to identify Malala's feelings during each of her opportunities to speak about girls' education, and analyze how the sequence of events impacted Malala.

Opportunity 1	How did this make Malala feel?
Malala gives a speech on Pashto TV (70–71).	Malala feel a bit sad when one of the schools gotted bombed
How was Malala's experience influenced by the circumstances in which she was living?	
Malala and her sibings have to sleep in their Parnets room and malala sleeps on the floor.	

Opportunity 2	How did this make Malala feel?
Malala writes a diary for the BBC (77–78).	
How was Malala's experience shaped or influenced by the previous opportunity?	

Opportunity 3	How did this make Malala feel?
The *New York Times* records Malala and her classmates on their last day of school (83).	
How was Malala's experience shaped or influenced by the previous opportunity?	

Name

Date Class

Handout 19B: Optional Fluency Practice 4

Directions:

1. Day 1: Read the text carefully and annotate to help you read fluently.
2. Each day:
   a. Practice reading the text aloud three to five times.
   b. Evaluate your progress by placing a checkmark in the appropriate, unshaded box.
   c. Ask someone (adult or peer) to listen and evaluate you as well.
3. Last day: Answer the self-reflection questions at the end.

"They cannot stop me. I will get my education," I told the cameraman. "If it is in home, school, or anyplace. This is our request to the world—save our schools, save our Pakistan, save our Swat." I sounded hopeful, but in my heart, I was worried. As my father looked at me, smiling uncomfortably with a mixture of pride and sadness for his daughter, I pictured myself stuck at home, reading whatever books I could find until I ran out of books. I was eleven years old. Was my schooling really going to end now? Was I going to end up like girls who quit school to cook and clean? What I didn't know was that my words would reach many ears. Some in distant parts of the world. Some right in Swat, in Taliban strongholds.

Yousafzai, Malala and Patricia McCormick. *I Am Malala: How One Girl Stood Up for Education and Changed the World*. Young Reader's Edition, Little, Brown and Company, 2014, p. 83.

Student Performance Checklist:	Day 1		Day 2		Day 3		Day 4	
	You	Listener*	You	Listener*	You	Listener*	You	Listener*
Accurately read the passage three to five times.								
Read with appropriate phrasing and pausing.								
Read with appropriate expression.								
Read articulately at a good pace and an audible volume.								

*Adult or peer

Self-reflection: What choices did you make when deciding how to read this passage, and why? What would you like to improve on or try differently next time? (*Thoughtfully answer these questions below.*)

Name

Date Class

Handout 19C: Style and Tone Revision

Directions: Analyze the style and tone of the passage. Revise the third paragraph to reflect a style and tone consistent with the first two paragraphs.

If she was afraid, I wouldn't do it. Because if I didn't have her support, it would be like speaking with only half my heart.

But my mother agreed. She gave us her answer with a verse from the Holy Quran. "Falsehood has to die," she said. "And truth has to come forward." God would protect me, she said, because my mission was a good one.

Many people in Swat saw danger everywhere they looked all around them, but our family did not at all look at life in that manner in any way. Whenever danger presented itself, we saw possibility, and we felt a responsibility to stand up for our homeland. My father and I are the optimistic ones who consistently say all the time that "Things have to get better." My mother is the stability underneath our feet, as she is our rock. While our heads are in the sky, her feet are on the ground, but we all believed in hope, and she has often said that "speaking up is the only way things will get better" (adapted from Yousafzai and McCormick 76).

Name

Date Class

Handout 20A: Challenges and Responses

Directions: Complete the table below, using evidence from the text. Then respond to the final questions.

Chapter Number	What challenges did Malala face in this chapter?	How did Malala respond to these challenges?
1		
4		
9		
12		
16		

1. Have Malala's challenges changed over the course of the text?

2. Have Malala's responses changed over the course of the text?

3. What does examining Malala's responses to challenges reveal about her?

Name

Date Class

Handout 20B: Essay Graphic Organizer

Directions: Use this planning document to outline your ideas before writing your research essay.

Introduction
Hook
Introduce
Thesis and Preview

Section 1: Hostile Environment

Heading:	
Topic **S**tatement:	
Evidence: Citation:	**E**laboration:
Evidence: Citation:	**E**laboration:
Evidence: Citation:	**E**laboration:
Concluding **S**tatement:	

Name

Date Class

Section 2: Heroic Actions

Heading:	
Topic Statement:	
Evidence: Citation:	**Elaboration:**
Evidence: Citation:	**Elaboration:**
Evidence: Citation:	**Elaboration:**
Concluding Statement:	

Section 3: Impacted Others Positively

(Can be combined with previous section or separate.)

Heading:	
Topic **S**tatement:	
Evidence: Citation:	**E**laboration:
Evidence: Citation:	**E**laboration:
Evidence: Citation:	**E**laboration:
Concluding Statement:	

Name

Date Class

Conclusion

Name

Date Class

Handout 21A: Central Ideas

Directions: With your partner, compare your ideas about the main ideas for each part in the text. Come to a consensus about what they are, and record them in the table below. Then, consider which ideas are central ideas throughout the three parts of the text.

What are the main ideas in part one?	Which are the central ideas of parts one through three?
What are the main ideas in part two?	
What are the main ideas in part three?	

Name

Date Class

Handout 21B: *-ive, -tive, -ative* Suffixes

Directions: Complete the table. Use a dictionary, if needed. Answer the final question individually.

Verb	Meaning	Adjective Using *-ive, -tive, -ative*	Definition of the Adjective
create			
		collaborative	
talk			
inform			
		preventative	

Describe what Malala was doing after school and while riding in the *dyna*. Incorporate two adjectives that use the *–ive*, *–tive*, or *–ative* suffix.

Name

Date Class

Handout 22A: Optional Focusing Question Task 3 Graphic Organizer

Directions: You may use this table to organize your thinking before composing your response to Focusing Question Task 3.

	How does this part fit into the overall structure of the text?	How does this part develop the text's central ideas?
Part One		
Part Two		

Part Three		
Part Four		

Name ______________________

Date ____________ Class ____________

Handout 23A: Source Integration

Directions: Read the original evidence and its use in the exemplar essay. Answer the questions using ideas from both texts.

Original Evidence from Source	EOM Task Exemplar 2
"Curiously enough it was Sir Ernest himself who rescued Holness. No doubt he was spending one of his usual wakeful nights and so was up and out in an instant. First he saved Holness's sleeping bag and then the man himself" (Orde-Lees).	In addition to creating order for his men, Shackleton was heroic because he took extraordinary and risky actions to save the lives of his crew. One of the men, Orde-Lees, describes a time when another crew member, Holness, was nearly crushed to death by cracking ice. Shackleton pulled Holness's sleeping bag out of the freezing water, and then managed to drag Holness and himself to safety. If Shackleton hadn't acted quickly, Holness would've been crushed to death by the ice.

1. Who is Orde-Lees? How does the author of the exemplar essay indicate who he is?

____

____

2. Underline the information in the Orde-Lees quote that the author didn't include in his or her evidence. Would including those ideas have made the evidence stronger? Why or why not?

____

____

3. Would the Orde-Lees evidence be more effective as a quote?

____

____

4. How does the elaboration of the Orde-Lees evidence connect the research to the topic statement?

Name ______________________

Date __________ Class __________

Handout 23B: Word Choice Analysis

Directions: Read passages A and B, and answer the questions below them.

A) But I looked at this Malala in the mirror with nothing but curiosity. I was like a scientist studying a specimen. I wanted to understand exactly what had happened, where the bullet went, what exactly it had done. I was ___________ by what I saw. (Yousafzai and McCormick 143)	B) I was also ___________with how we would pay for all this. Whenever I saw the doctors and nurses talking to each other, I thought for sure that they were saying, "Malala doesn't have any money. Malala can't pay for her treatment." There was one doctor who always looked sad, so I wrote him a note. *Why are you sad?* I asked. I thought it was because he knew I couldn't pay. But he replied, "I'm not sad." (Yousafzai and McCormick 140)
1. Which word belongs in the blank, *obsessed* or *fascinated*?	1. Which word belongs in the blank, *obsessed* or *fascinated*?
2. Identify one to two words in the passage that helped you know which word fit best. Explain how this word/these words served as a clue as to which word belonged in the blank.	2. Identify one to two words in the passage that helped you know which word fit best. Explain how this word/these words served as a clue as to which word belonged in the blank.

Consider what Malala is obsessed with and what she's only fascinated by. What does this tell you about what's important to her?

____

____

____

____

Name

Date Class

Handout 24A: Event Organizer

Directions: Using chapters 26, 27, and 29, organize the events from Malala's shooting to her reunion with her family in Birmingham.

	Malala	Malala's family	Dr. Javid and Dr. Fiona
The hours after the shooting			"In Pakistan advising army doctors on how to set up a liver-transplant system" (149).
Two days after the shooting			
At the hospital in Rawalpindi	"Developed an infection...[her] condition had started to worsen" (149).		
At the hospital in Birmingham			

Name

Date Class

Handout 24B: Effective Evidence Integration

Directions: Complete the missing elements of the paragraph.

<table>
<tr><td colspan="2">Heading: Taking On the Unknown</td></tr>
<tr><td colspan="2">Topic Statement:
Because he knew it was critical to get help quickly, Shackleton and two of his men took incredible risks and endangered their lives to reach the whaling station in thirty-six hours.</td></tr>
<tr><td>Introduction of Source:</td><td rowspan="2">Elaboration:</td></tr>
<tr><td>Evidence:
At one point, Shackleton and his men slid down a mountain into unknown territory, risking possible death.
Citation: (Armstrong)</td></tr>
<tr><td colspan="2">Concluding Statement:
It was amazing that Shackleton and his two crew members were able to cross South Georgia Island at all, but it was miraculous that they did it in less than two days. Their incredible efforts undoubtedly saved the lives of the rest of the crew.</td></tr>
</table>

Name

Date Class

Handout 24C: Frayer Model

Directions: Complete the Frayer Model for the word *ordeal*.

Definition:	**Characteristics:**
Examples:	**Non-Examples:**

Word:

ordeal

Name

Date Class

Handout 25A: Word Choice Analysis

Directions: Consult a dictionary to determine the meanings of *chaotic* and *perplexed*, adding their definitions to the New Words section of your Vocabulary Journal. Read the two passages below, and answer the questions that follow.

A) "I missed home terribly. I missed my school friends, I missed the mountains, the waterfall, the beautiful Swat River, and the lush green fields. I even missed the messy, ________ streets of Mingora" (Yousafzai and McCormick 173).	B) "My mother, who cannot speak English like the rest of us, wanders ________ through the shops, inspecting the strange foods for sale" (Yousafzai and McCormick 176).
1. Which word belongs in the blank, *chaotic* or *perplexed*?	1. Which word belongs in the blank, *chaotically* or *perplexed*?
2. Identify one to two words in the passage that helped you know which word fit best. Explain how this word/these words served as a clue as to which word belonged in the blank.	2. Identify one to two words in the sentence that helped you know which word fit best. Explain how this word/these words served as a clue as to which word belonged in the blank.

Taking into account what you understand about *chaotic* and *perplexed*, describe one way in which Malala or her mother are learning to adjust to their new environment.

Name

Date Class

Handout 26A: Central Ideas

Directions: Use the ideas on Handout 15A to determine the main ideas in parts four and five. Then, consider whether the central ideas have changed at all since you completed Handout 21A or if new central ideas of *I Am Malala* have emerged; use these ideas to complete the final column.

What are the main ideas in part four?	Which are the central ideas of this text?
▪ ______ ▪ ______ ▪ ______ ▪ ______	▪ ______ ▪ ______ ▪ ______ ▪ ______
What are the main ideas in part five?	
▪ ______ ▪ ______ ▪ ______ ▪ ______	

Name

Date Class

Handout 26B: Malala Yousafzai Exemplar

Directions: Use the following exemplar essay as directed and to support your completion of the EOM Task.

An Extraordinary Girl

Can you imagine waking up one day and being told that you cannot go to school anymore? For many kids, this seems like a dream come true. Now imagine that the reason you can't go to school is because militant terrorists have taken over your city and don't think you have a right to learn. Now how would you feel? For Malala Yousafzai, this unjust situation happened. Malala was living in Mingora, in the Swat valley of Pakistan, when the Taliban seized control of the region. They declared that girls should not go to school and enforced this demand by using violence. In response to this threat, Malala acted heroically. She acted on behalf of other girls by speaking out against the Taliban's declaration, and she took extraordinary risks to her own safety to do so. These actions had a great impact, exposing what was happening in Pakistan and raising global awareness of how difficult it was for girls to get an education.

A Place of Violence

When the Taliban came to Swat in 2007, Malala's environment became incredibly hostile. According to *Scope* author Kristen Lewis, the militants "blew up government buildings and murdered police officers" (Lewis 6). No one felt safe when they realized that their government and police force could no longer protect them. Malala was often kept awake at night by the sounds of gunshots. As she walked to school, she would pass the bodies of people who were murdered by the Taliban (Lewis 6). These bodies were reminders of what happened to those who didn't follow the Taliban's laws. They made Malala fear for her own life and the lives of those she cared about. The Taliban used violence and terror to control the people of Swat.

A Heroic Response

Malala responded to the hostile environment in Mingora by speaking out on behalf of all girls even though this action threatened her safety. After the Taliban declared that girls had no right to education, attendance at Malala's school dropped by "more than 60 percent," but Malala kept attending even though it meant risking her life (Lewis 6). Malala was determined not to give in to the Taliban's orders. This courageous action inspired other young girls to keep attending school. Malala did not stop there and took every opportunity she could to draw attention to the need for girls' education. For example, she revealed to the world what was happening to girls in her city by writing an anonymous online diary ("Profile: Malala Yousafzai"). As her confidence grew, she "appeared in a *New York Times* documentary, went on television shows, and gave powerful speeches to Pakistani kids" (Lewis 8). In all of these appearances, she spoke about how all children have a right to an education. She even spoke to Richard Holbrooke, who was the U.S. special envoy in Pakistan at the time, and urged him to "do something about the state of affairs for women who want an education" ("Profile: Malala Yousafzai"). Unfortunately, by speaking out, Malala and her family were constantly threatened by the Taliban, and eventually Malala was shot and almost killed. But Malala refused to be silenced by violence and continued to advocate for girls' education.

Making a Difference

Malala's heroic actions of speaking out and not being intimidated by the Taliban have resulted in more and more people becoming involved in the universal campaign for girls' education. For example, when Malala was recovering in the hospital, one million people signed a petition asking the Pakistani government "to make a place in school for every girl" (Lewis 9). Her actions helped raise awareness about the unequal treatment girls face not only in Pakistan but around the world. Malala was able to use her fame to create a foundation dedicated to making her dream a reality. This foundation, the Malala Fund, began after her shooting and it "helps children in education around the world" ("Profile: Malala Yousafzai"). After nearly losing her life, Malala did not retire from activism but instead continues to devote herself to improving the lives of children in her country and around the world.

Malala is an ordinary person who responded to a hostile environment in an extraordinary way. She considered the cause of girls' education more important than her own life. This created a movement that has steadily become more powerful. Malala reminds us of the powerful impact one person can make when they are willing to stand up for others and a cause greater than themselves.

Works Cited

Lewis, Kristen. "Malala the Powerful: The Amazing True Story of a 15-Year-old Girl Who Stood Up to a Deadly Terrorist Group." *Scope*, Scholastic, Sept. 2013, Web. Web. Accessed 2 Nov. 2015.

"Profile: Malala Yousafzai." *BBC News*, BBC, 10 Dec. 2014, Web. Accessed 2 Nov. 2015.

Yousafzai, Malala, and Patricia McCormick. *I Am Malala: How One Girl Stood Up for Education and Changed the World*. Young Reader's Edition, Little, Brown and Company, 2014.

Name

Date Class

Handout 26C: Four Square Organizer

Directions: Complete the Four Square Organizer for the word *campaign* and answer the question on the next page.

Definition:	**Characteristics:**
What are the relationships among dreams, beliefs, and *campaigns*?	**What are the differences among dreams, beliefs, and *campaigns*?**

Word:

campaign

"So, yes, the Taliban have shot me. But they can only shoot a body. They cannot shoot my dreams, they cannot kill my beliefs, and they cannot stop my *campaign* to see every girl and every boy in school" (Yousafzai and McCormick 188).

How does the phrase "cannot stop my *campaign*" (188) impact the meaning of this statement?

Name

Date Class

Handout 27A: Optional Informative/Explanatory Essay Graphic Organizer

Directions: You may use these graphic organizers to help you plan your explanatory essay for Focusing Question Task 4.

Introduction
Hook
Introduce
Thesis and Preview

Supporting Paragraph	
Topic **S**tatement:	
Evidence: Citation:	**E**laboration:
Evidence: Citation:	**E**laboration:
Concluding Statement:	

Name

Date Class

Supporting Paragraph	
Topic **S**tatement:	
Evidence: Citation:	**E**laboration:
Evidence: Citation:	**E**laboration:
Concluding Statement:	

Conclusion

Name

Date Class

Handout 28A: Claims and Reasoning

Directions: As you listen to Malala's speech, record the claims she makes and the reasoning she gives to support her claims.

Claim	Reasoning

Read the transcript of the speech on Handout 28B, annotating any claims or reasoning you missed. Evaluate your ability to listen for the claims and reasoning, circling one of the options below:

3: I identified all of the claims and reasoning to support them.

2: I identified some of the claims and reasoning to support them.

1: I was unable to identify a claim and/or the reasoning to support the claim.

What was one of the challenges you experienced while noting claims and evidences during the speech?

Name

Date Class

Handout 28B: "Malala Yousafzai - Nobel Lecture"

Directions: Use this transcript as instructed after listening to Malala's speech.

Bismillah hir rahman ir rahim.
In the name of God, the most merciful, the most beneficent.

Your Majesties, Your Royal Highnesses, distinguished members of the Norwegian Nobel Committee,

Dear sisters and brothers, today is a day of great happiness for me. I am humbled that the Nobel Committee has selected me for this precious award.

Thank you to everyone for your continued support and love. Thank you for the letters and cards that I still receive from all around the world. Your kind and encouraging words strengthens and inspires me.

I would like to thank my parents for their unconditional love. Thank you to my father for not clipping my wings and for letting me fly. Thank you to my mother for inspiring me to be patient and to always speak the truth–which we strongly believe is the true message of Islam. And also thank you to all my wonderful teachers, who inspired me to believe in myself and be brave.

I am proud, well in fact, I am very proud to be the first Pashtun, the first Pakistani, and the youngest person to receive this award. Along with that, along with that, I am pretty certain that I am also the first recipient of the Nobel Peace Prize who still fights with her younger brothers. I want there to be peace everywhere, but my brothers and I are still working on that.

I am also honored to receive this award together with Kailash Satyarthi, who has been a champion for children's rights for a long time. Twice as long, in fact, than I have been alive. I am proud that we can work together, we can work together and show the world that an Indian and a Pakistani, they can work together and achieve their goals of children's rights.

Dear brothers and sisters, I was named after the inspirational Malalai of Maiwand who is the Pashtun Joan of Arc. The word *Malala* means "grief stricken," "sad," but in order to lend some happiness to it, my grandfather would always call me "Malala–the happiest girl in the world," and today I am very happy that we are together fighting for an important cause.

This award is not just for me. It is for those forgotten children who want education. It is for those frightened children who want peace. It is for those voiceless children who want change.

I am here to stand up for their rights, to raise their voice… it is not time to pity them. It is not time to pity them. It is time to take action so it becomes the last time, the last time, so it becomes the last time that we see a child deprived of education.

I have found that people describe me in many different ways.

Some people call me the girl who was shot by the Taliban.

And some, the girl who fought for her rights.

Some people, call me a "Nobel Laureate" now.

However, my brothers still call me that annoying bossy sister. As far as I know, I am just a committed and even stubborn person who wants to see every child getting quality education, who wants to see women having equal rights and who wants peace in every corner of the world.

Education is one of the blessings of life—and one of its necessities. That has been my experience during the 17 years of my life. In my paradise home, Swat, I always loved learning and discovering new things. I remember when my friends and I would decorate our hands with henna on special occasions. And instead of drawing flowers and patterns we would paint our hands with mathematical formulas and equations.

We had a thirst for education, we had a thirst for education because our future was right there in that classroom. We would sit and learn and read together. We loved to wear neat and tidy school uniforms and we would sit there with big dreams in our eyes. We wanted to make our parents proud and prove that we could also excel in our studies and achieve those goals, which some people think only boys can.

But things did not remain the same. When I was in Swat, which was a place of tourism and beauty, suddenly changed into a place of terrorism. I was just ten that more than 400 schools were destroyed. Women were flogged. People were killed. And our beautiful dreams turned into nightmares.

Education went from being a right to being a crime.

Girls were stopped from going to school.

When my world suddenly changed, my priorities changed too.

I had two options. One was to remain silent and wait to be killed. And the second was to speak up and then be killed.

Name

Date Class

I chose the second one. I decided to speak up.

We could not just stand by and see those injustices of the terrorists denying our rights, ruthlessly killing people and misusing the name of Islam. We decided to raise our voice and tell them: Have you not learnt, have you not learnt that in the Holy Quran Allah says: if you kill one person it is as if you kill the whole humanity?

Do you not know that Mohammad, peace be upon him, the prophet of mercy, he says, “do not harm yourself or others”?

And do you not know that the very first word of the Holy Quran is the word *Iqra*, which means “read”?

The terrorists tried to stop us and attacked me and my friends who are here today, on our school bus in 2012, but neither their ideas nor their bullets could win.

We survived. And since that day, our voices have grown louder and louder.

I tell my story, not because it is unique, but because it is not.

It is the story of many girls.

Today, I tell their stories too. I have brought with me some of my sisters from Pakistan, from Nigeria and from Syria, who share this story. My brave sisters Shazia and Kainat who were also shot that day on our school bus. But they have not stopped learning. And my brave sister Kainat Soomro who went through severe abuse and extreme violence, even her brother was killed, but she did not succumb.

Also my sisters here, whom I have met during my Malala Fund campaign. My 16-year-old courageous sister, Mezon from Syria, who now lives in Jordan as refugee and goes from tent to tent encouraging girls and boys to learn. And my sister Amina, from the North of Nigeria, where Boko Haram threatens, and stops girls and even kidnaps girls, just for wanting to go to school.

Though I appear as one girl, though I appear as one girl, one person, who is 5 foot 2 inches tall, if you include my high heels. (It means I am 5 foot only.) I am not a lone voice, I am not a lone voice, I am many.

I am Malala. But I am also Shazia.

I am Kainat.

I am Kainat Soomro.

I am Mezon.

I am Amina. I am those 66 million girls who are deprived of education. And today I am not raising my voice, it is the voice of those 66 million girls.

Sometimes people like to ask me why should girls go to school, why is it important for them. But I think the more important question is why shouldn't they, why shouldn't they have this right to go to school.

Dear sisters and brothers, today, in half of the world, we see rapid progress and development. However, there are many countries where millions still suffer from the very old problems of war, poverty, and injustice.

We still see conflicts in which innocent people lose their lives and children become orphans. We see many people becoming refugees in Syria, Gaza and Iraq. In Afghanistan, we see families being killed in suicide attacks and bomb blasts.

Many children in Africa do not have access to education because of poverty. And as I said, we still see, we still see girls who have no freedom to go to school in the north of Nigeria.

Many children in countries like Pakistan and India, as Kailash Satyarthi mentioned, many children, especially in India and Pakistan are deprived of their right to education because of social taboos, or they have been forced into child marriage or into child labour.

One of my very good school friends, the same age as me, who had always been a bold and confident girl, dreamed of becoming a doctor. But her dream remained a dream. At the age of 12, she was forced to get married. And then soon she had a son, she had a child when she herself was still a child—only 14. I know that she could have been a very good doctor.

But she couldn't...because she was a girl.

Her story is why I dedicate the Nobel Peace Prize money to the Malala Fund, to help give girls quality education, everywhere, anywhere in the world and to raise their voices. The first place this funding will go to is where my heart is, to build schools in Pakistan—especially in my home of Swat and Shangla.

In my own village, there is still no secondary school for girls. And it is my wish and my commitment, and now my challenge to build one so that my friends and my sisters can go there to school and get quality education and to get this opportunity to fulfil their dreams.

This is where I will begin, but it is not where I will stop. I will continue this fight until I see every child, every child in school.

Name

Date Class

Dear brothers and sisters, great people, who brought change, like **Martin Luther King** and **Nelson Mandela**, **Mother Teresa** and **Aung San Suu Kyi**, once stood here on this stage. I hope the steps that Kailash Satyarthi and I have taken so far and will take on this journey will also bring change–lasting change.

My great hope is that this will be **the last time**, this will be the last time we must fight for education. Let's solve this once and for all.

We have already taken many steps. Now it is time to take a leap.

It is not time to tell the world leaders to realise how important education is–they already know it–their own children are in good schools. Now it is time to call them to take action for the rest of the world's children.

We ask the world leaders to unite and make education their top priority.

Fifteen years ago, the world leaders decided on a set of global goals, the Millennium Development Goals. In the years that have followed, we have seen some progress. The number of children out of school has been halved, as Kailash Satyarthi said. However, the world focused only on primary education, and progress did not reach everyone.

In year 2015, representatives from all around the world will meet in the **United Nations** to set the next set of goals, the Sustainable Development Goals. This will set the world's ambition for the next generations.

The world can no longer accept, the world can no longer accept that basic education is enough. Why do leaders accept that for children in developing countries, only basic literacy is sufficient, when their own children do homework in Algebra, Mathematics, Science and Physics?

Leaders must seize this opportunity to guarantee a free, quality, primary and secondary education for every child.

Some will say this is impractical, or too expensive, or too hard. Or maybe even impossible. But it is time the world thinks bigger.

Dear sisters and brothers, the so-called world of adults may understand it, but we children don't. Why is it that countries which we call "strong" are so powerful in creating wars but are so weak in bringing peace? Why is it that giving guns is so easy but giving books is so hard? Why is it, why is it that making tanks is so easy, but building schools is so hard?

We are living in the modern age and we believe that nothing is impossible. We have reached the moon 45 years ago and maybe will soon land on Mars. Then, in this 21st century, we must be able to give every child quality education.

Dear sisters and brothers, dear fellow children, we must work… not wait. Not just the politicians and the world leaders, we all need to contribute. Me. You. We. It is our duty.

Let us become the first generation to decide to be the last, let us become the first generation that decides to be the last that sees empty classrooms, lost childhoods, and wasted potentials.

Let this be the **last time** that a girl or a boy spends their childhood in a factory.

Let this be the last time that a girl is forced into early child marriage.

Let this be the last time that a child loses life in war.

Let this be the last time that we see a child out of school.

Let this end with us.

Let's begin this ending ... together ... today ... right here, right now. Let's begin this ending now.

Thank you so much.

Yousafzai, Malala. "Malala Yousafzai – Nobel Lecture." *Nobelprize.org*, Nobel Media AB, 10 Dec. 2014, Web. Accessed 6 Dec. 2016.

Name

Date Class

Handout 29A: Peer Content Review

Directions: Read your partner's essay and then complete the Peer Content Review. Be detailed in your responses.

Content Review	
Writer of Essay	Reviewer of Essay
1. Does the **introduction** contain a **hook**? An **introduction** that includes context about the individual? A **thesis** that conveys your essential idea? A **preview** of the supporting points? Underline and label each part of the introduction on the draft. How could the introduction be improved?	
2. Does each **body paragraph** have a **topic statement**? Circle the topic statement in each paragraph. Does this topic statement align with the individual's environment (E), his or her heroic action (A), or their positive impact on others (I)? Annotate the alignment of each topic statement by writing the letter next to it. Could the focus of the topic statement be clearer? How could it better support the thesis?	

3. Is textual evidence included and cited in **each body paragraph**? Is the evidence relevant? Sufficient? Does it support the topic statement? How could it be improved?
4. Does **each body paragraph** provide thorough elaboration of the evidence provided? Underline where you see elaboration. How could it be improved? Overall, does this paragraph develop either the individual's environment, his or her actions, or his or her impact? How could it be improved?
5. Is there a **concluding** paragraph? Does it reinforce the thesis and supporting points? Does it contain the "So What?"? How could the conclusion be improved?

Name

Date Class

6. Is there a **Works Cited** section? Is there an author, title, date, and publisher or web link listed for each source?

7. Are there **headings** to organize the content? How could the headings be improved?

Name

Date Class

Handout 29B: Peer Style and Conventions Edit

Directions: Use this tool to provide feedback on style and conventions.

Style and Conventions Editing		
	Yes	*No*
1. Do all the pronouns have **clear antecedents**?		
How could this be improved?		
2. Does the author maintain a **consistent style**?		
How could this be improved?		
3. Does the author maintain a **consistent tone**?		
How could this be improved?		
4. How effectively does the narrative follow the **conventions** of standard written English? Note where you see errors in conventions, spelling, punctuation, or grammar.		

Name

Date Class

Handout 30A: "The Golden Hoard: An Ancient Afghan Treasure Is Recovered"

Directions: Use this text as directed on Assessment 30A: New-Read Assessment 2. Both the paragraphs and the lines have been numbered for ease of use, and definitions for the highlighted words have been provided in the footnotes.

1 A two-thousand-year-old Afghan treasure has come to light after a quarter century of rumors, legends, and speculation[1]. Ibex figurines and jeweled scabbards and golden beasts—nearly twenty-one-thousand pieces in all—have been found again.

2 Precisely where the treasure is, Afghan officials aren't saying in the interests of security. The gold hoard from the ancient kingdom of Bactria has survived the years of chaos since it was discovered: the Soviet invasion, the warring among the *mujahideen*, and the rise of the Taliban. Stories circulated that the golden objects had been carried off to Moscow, or sold on the black market, or melted down. In one account, just before the American forces arrived in 2001, the Taliban ran out of time trying to blow the central bank's vault. No one could say for sure what had happened.

3 Then in August of 2003, the government of Afghanistan announced that the Bactrian gold had been found and invited archaeologist Fred Hiebert to verify the fact. "I went over there to try and find out whether there was any truth to this rumor that the Bactrian gold was safe," says Hiebert, a specialist in ancient trade in Central Asia. "We were invited to inventory what collections they had, systematically, and do a verification."

4 Hiebert held the original field notes from the excavation by Russian archaeologist Viktor Sarianidi in the 1970s. With support from the NEH and the National Geographic Society, he and museum specialist Carla Grissmann were in Afghanistan last summer to conduct an inventory. The treasure, they determined, was intact.

5 The artifacts were uncovered in 1978 in the Mound of Gold, or Tillya Tepe, in a northern Afghan province that lies between the Hindu Kush Mountains and the Amu Darya River. The site was rumored to contain a golden man buried in a coffin of gold. Instead, Sarianidi's team found a four-thousand-year-old temple, and within its walls, the tombs of five women and one man. The archaeologists speculated that sometime during the first century C.E., a tribe of Bactrian nomads[2] had hidden the graves within the ruins of the abandoned temple.

---

1. *speculation:* the act of wondering or guessing
2. *nomads:* people with no permanent home, who travel from place to place

Each person was interred[3] with a dazzling array of jewelry, beads, buckles, coins, 6
mirrors, and gold plaques that had trimmed their clothing—which, as was the nomadic tradition, the nobles had worn or carried with them in life. Four of the six nomads were buried with their heads facing north. Coins were placed in the mouths of two of the women: the toll for Charon to ferry them across the river Styx.

The necropolis[4] dates from a time in Bactria about which little is known. "We call it a 7
dark period in history, because it's very hard to find archaeological remains of these people," Hiebert says. "They have some dwellings, but they tend to be small. It's hard to get a handle on who the nomads were. So we can use this set of artifacts to help us understand what role they might have had in Silk Road trade, and what role they might have had in terms of the melding[5] of cultures in this area."

Opening the safes that held the ancient treasure was no easy matter. In Afghan tradition, 8
a *talwildar*, or key holder, takes responsibility for guarding a treasure, passing on the charge to the next generation. "He is bonded. The man with the key has pledged his family house, his land, if he has any land. His son will inherit the keys," says Grissmann.

Any safe, trunk, or vault, regardless of the number of locks it possesses, is also sealed 9
with a piece of paper bearing the signatures of witnesses, all of whom are required to be present when the paper is slit and the locks reopened. The national museum has employed this process for decades, and it was by this same method that the museum accepted Sarianidi's find.

"This was a ritual that was performed every day at the Kabul Museum when I was 10
working there," says Grissmann, who began working for the museum in 1973. "Every night at the Kabul Museum there was a procession—the people that signed, three witnesses, and the man with the glue pot. And the same thing every morning. The three people paraded down, opening each exhibition room. Each showcase had a little padlock with a piece of paper signed."

For the inventory of the Bactrian this year inside the Central Bank, five bank officials 11
were needed to open the vault. But the *talwildar* required to open the safes containing the ancient collection had disappeared years ago and no one knew what had become of him or any member of his family. After much debate, the president of Afghanistan made a highly unusual decision, decreeing that a judge from the ministry of justice would be

3. *interred:* buried
4. *necropolis:* burial place
5. *melding:* blend or mix

Name

Date Class

allowed as a substitute *talwildar*. The safes were cracked open, and the inventory was able to commence[6].

Inside the six safes was the entire Bactrian hoard, intact, just as Sarianidi had left it 12
twenty-five years ago. Gold figurines, diadems[7] adorned by trees with birds perching in them, jewel-encrusted daggers, scabbards, and buckles; silver Chinese mirrors, ivory Indian combs, leopards, panthers, griffins, and other beasts designed in chalcedony, turquoise, agate, and cornelian; gold shoe buckles encrusted in turquoise, depicting dragon-drawn chariots; and heavy pendant earrings bearing a scene in which a ruler struggles with a fierce dragon, in a fusion[8] of Persian, Achaemenian, and Eurasian Scythian styles.

The nomads had been buried with every manner of rich adornment, from gold cutouts 13
sewn to the bottoms of their shoes, to a collapsible, finely worked gold crown that could be packed up easily. In his account of the excavation, *The Golden Hoard of Bactria*, Sarianidi speculates: "Could it be so that, considering the nomad's traditional way of life, the crown could be safely stowed away in a saddlebag, without fear of damaging it during long treks or military campaigns?"

In the inventory last summer, Hiebert and Grissmann worked for thirty-six days, eight 14
hours each day, alongside eighteen members of the museum staff and under the eye of bank officials, security guards, and representatives from each ministry.

To preserve the Afghan *talwildar* tradition, Hiebert devised a new curatorial process. 15
The judge, acting as the Bactrian gold's *talwildar*, would remove an object and hand it to Hiebert, who measured and weighed it and assigned it a new number. It was described in English and in Dari and photographed digitally. The photographs were printed on the spot, attached to the English-Dari information sheets, signed by a new *talwildar*, and placed in a new safe alongside the object. Copies of the inventories were given to the museum, the ministry of justice, and other institutions.

"For me, what's interesting about this system, which I respect deeply, is that it has 16
transcended[9] the different administrations that they've had in Afghanistan," says Hiebert. "There were *talwildars* during the king's days. There were *talwildars* during the Taliban times. There were *talwildars* during the Soviet period."

---

6. *commence*: begin
7. *diadems*: royal crowns or headbands
8. *fusion*: combination
9. *transcended*: survived and continued

"I wanted to make sure that by introducing modern museum curation we weren't disrupting that system," he continues. "That was perhaps one of the most complex things that we had to do…" 17

Excerpt from:

Galvin, Rachel. "The Golden Hoard: An Ancient Afghan Treasure Is Recovered." Humanities, vol. 25, no. 6, Nov./Dec. 2004, pp. 11–16, Web. Accessed 6 Dec. 2016.

Name

Date Class

Handout 30B: Informative/Explanatory Writing Checklist

Directions: Use this checklist to revise your writing. Mark + for "yes" and Δ for "not yet." Ask someone (adult or peer) to evaluate your writing as well.

Reading Comprehension	**Self** +/Δ	**Peer** +/Δ	**Teacher** +/Δ
I cite textual evidence to support my analysis.			
I cite textual evidence to support my inferences.			
Structure			
I respond to all parts of the prompt.			
I focus on my topic throughout the piece.			
I introduce my individual clearly and give context about them in my introduction paragraph.			
My introduction paragraph gives some kind of preview of the rest of the piece.			
I organize my ideas clearly in body paragraphs.			
My conclusion paragraph supports the focus.			
I use transitions to smoothly and logically connect paragraphs and ideas.			
Development			
I develop my topic with sufficient evidence from text(s).			
My evidence is relevant to the topic.			
I elaborate upon evidence by analyzing it accurately.			
Style			
I use a variety of sentence patterns (simple, compound, complex, compound-complex) to add clarity and interest to my writing.			
I use vocabulary words that are specific and appropriate to the content.			
I write precisely and concisely, without using unnecessary words.			
I write in an appropriately formal style.			
My writing style is appropriate for the audience.			

Conventions			
I use specific pronouns to make my meaning clear.			
My style and tone are consistent throughout my essay.			
Research			
I draw on several credible sources for relevant information to support my thesis statement and ideas.			
I quote, summarize, or paraphrase the information from my sources.			
I cite each source used within my essay.			
I provide bibliographic information about each of my sources in a Works Cited section at the end of my essay.			
Writing Process			
I develop and strengthen my writing through planning, revising, and working with a peer.			
Total number of +'s			

Name

Date Class

Handout 30C: Informative/Explanatory Writing Rubric

Directions: Refer to the Informative/Explanatory Writing Rubric to guide your End-of-Module Task.

	4 (Exceeds expectations)	3 (Meets expectations)	2 (Partially meets expectations)	1 (Does not yet meet expectations)
Structure	▪ Responds thoroughly to all elements of prompt ▪ Maintains focus on topic throughout piece ▪ Introduces topic ▪ Organizes ideas clearly and effectively ▪ Provides a strong conclusion that follows from and expands on the focus ▪ Uses appropriate transitions to clarify relationships	▪ Responds to all elements of prompt ▪ Maintains focus on topic throughout piece with occasional minor departures ▪ Introduces topic ▪ Organizes ideas clearly and effectively ▪ Provides a conclusion that follows from the focus ▪ Uses appropriate transitions to clarify relationships	▪ Responds to some elements of prompt ▪ Often departs from focus on topic ▪ Introduces topic in an incomplete or unclear way ▪ Organizes ideas inconsistently ▪ Provides a conclusion that is incomplete or may not follow from the focus ▪ Inconsistently uses transitions to connect ideas	▪ Does not respond to prompt; off-topic ▪ Piece lacks focus on topic ▪ Does not introduce topic ▪ Ideas are disorganized ▪ Does not provide a conclusion ▪ Does not use transitions to connect ideas
Development	▪ Develops topic with relevant, sufficient evidence from texts(s) ▪ Elaborates upon evidence thoroughly with accurate, insightful analysis	▪ Develops topic with sufficient, relevant evidence from text(s) ▪ Elaborates upon evidence with accurate analysis	▪ Develops topic with insufficient relevant evidence from texts(s) ▪ Elaborates upon evidence vaguely or superficially	▪ Does not use relevant evidence from text(s) ▪ Does not elaborate upon evidence
Style	▪ Varies sentence patterns for clarity, interest, emphasis, and style ▪ Uses precise language and domain-specific vocabulary ▪ Consistently expresses ideas precisely ▪ Establishes and maintains a consistent, formal, and engaging style ▪ Writing shows exceptional awareness and skill in addressing audience's needs	▪ Varies sentence patterns for clarity and interest ▪ Uses domain-specific vocabulary ▪ Mostly expresses ideas precisely ▪ Establishes a formal style, with occasional minor lapses ▪ Writing is appropriate to audience	▪ Varies sentence patterns occasionally for clarity or interest ▪ Uses general vocabulary with a few domain-specific words ▪ Language is occasionally precise and may be unnecessarily wordy ▪ Attempts to use a formal style but with many lapses ▪ Writing is somewhat appropriate to audience	▪ Sentence patterns are basic and repetitive ▪ Uses limited vocabulary inappropriate to the content ▪ Language is imprecise and lacks concision, often wordy or redundant ▪ Uses an inappropriately informal style ▪ Writing is inappropriate to audience

Conventions	▪ Shows strong command of grammar, mechanics, spelling, and usage; errors are minor and few	▪ Shows consistent command of grammar, mechanics, spelling, and usage; occasional errors do not significantly interfere with meaning	▪ Shows inconsistent command of grammar, mechanics, spelling, and usage; some errors interfere with meaning	▪ Does not show command of grammar, mechanics, spelling, and usage; errors significantly interfere with overall meaning and writing is difficult to follow

Volume of Reading Reflection Questions

Courage in Crisis, Grade 6, Module 4

Student Name: ______________________________

Text: ______________________________

Author: ______________________________

Topic: ______________________________

Genre/type of book: ______________________________

Directions: Share your knowledge by answering the questions below.

Informational Text:

1. **Wonder:** Reading only the title, the cover illustration, and the back matter, jot down three things you noticed and three questions that stem from your observations.

2. **Organize:** Summarize a central idea of the text and its supporting details, including any details about enduring hostile environments and heroism.

3. **Reveal:** Choose an interesting sentence in the text. Explain how that sentence fits into the overall structure of the text. Explain how it develops the big idea of that section or the whole text.

4. **Distill:** What is the essential meaning of this text? What does this tell you about the author's point of view? What does it tell you about the author's purpose in writing this text?

5. **Know:** What is the most important information you gained from this text? Describe how this information might be different if it had been presented from a different, or even opposite, point of view.

6. **Vocabulary**: Write and define three important vocabulary words that you learned in this

text. What are the context clues that helped you to know their meanings?

Literary Text:

1. **Wonder:** What drew your attention to this text? How do you think the story might connect to the module theme, "Courage in Crisis?"

2. **Organize:** Write a short retelling of the story in the form of a cartoon. Try to retell the story in five frames. Use the cartoon to share a summary with a friend or adult.

3. **Reveal:** Describe how the setting of this story impacts the plot. How would this story have been altered if there were a completely different setting?

4. **Distill:** What is a theme of this story? How does the theme of this story compare or c ontrast to the theme in another story you read this year?

5. **Know:** What have you learned about heroism through this piece of fiction?

6. **Vocabulary:** Identify three words or phrases that require the reader to understand figurative language. Explain the intended meaning of the word or phrase in context.

Wit & Wisdom Parent Tip Sheet

WHAT IS MY GRADE 6 STUDENT LEARNING IN MODULE 4?

Wit & Wisdom is our English curriculum. It builds knowledge of key topics in history, science, and literature through the study of excellent texts. By reading and responding to literature and nonfiction texts, we build knowledge of the following topics:

Module 1: Resilience in the Great Depression

Module 2: A Hero's Journey

Module 3: Narrating the Unknown

Module 4: Courage in Crisis

In the fourth module, *Courage in Crisis*, students work across multiple texts to construct a complex understanding of what it means to endure hostile environments and respond heroically to positively impact others. We will ask the question: *How can the challenges of a hostile environment inspire heroism?*

OUR CLASS WILL READ THESE TEXTS:

Historical Account (Informational)

- *Shipwreck at the Bottom of the World: The Extraordinary True Story of Shackleton and the Endurance*, Jennifer Armstrong

Memoir

- *I Am Malala: How One Girl Stood Up for Education and Changed the World*, Malala Yousafzai and Patricia McCormick

OUR CLASS WILL EXAMINE THIS PAINTING:

- *Snow Storm: Steam-Boat off a Harbour's Mouth*, Joseph Mallord William Turner

OUR CLASS WILL READ THIS ARTICLE:

- "The Golden Hoard: An Ancient Afghan Treasure Is Recovered," Rachel Galvin

OUR CLASS WILL ANALYZE THIS ARTIFACT:

- Bactrian Gold Crown

OUR CLASS WILL VIEW THESE VIDEOS:

- *Lost Treasures of Afghanistan*, National Geographic
- "Malala Yousafzai Nobel Peace Prize Speech," Malala Fund

OUR CLASS WILL ASK THESE QUESTIONS:

- How do Shackleton and his crew respond to the hostile environment of Antarctica?
- How does Armstrong's portrayal of Shackleton and his crew develop the concept of heroism?
- How do Malala and her community respond to the hostile environment in Pakistan?
- How does Yousafzai's and McCormick's portrayal of Malala develop the concept of heroism?

QUESTIONS TO ASK AT HOME:

As your Grade 6 student reads, ask:

- *How does this text build your knowledge of heroism? Share what you know about responding to the challenges of hostile environments.*

BOOKS TO READ AT HOME:

- *Amelia Lost: The Life and Disappearance of Amelia Earhart*, Candace Fleming
- *Unbroken: A World War II Story of Survival, Resilience, and Redemption*, Laura Hillenbrand
- *Trapped: How the World Rescued 33 Miners from 2,000 Feet Below the Chilean Desert*, Marc Aronson
- *Freedom Walkers: The Story of the Montgomery Bus Boycott*, Russell Freedman
- *Shackleton's Stowaway*, Victoria McKernan
- *Swiss Family Robinson*, Johann David Wyss
- *Journey to the Center of the Earth*, Jules Verne
- *Shipwrecked: Adventures of a Japanese Boy*, Rhonda Blumberg
- *Helen's Eyes: A Photobiography of Annie Sullivan, Helen Keller's Teacher*, Marfe Ferguson Delano
- *Candy Bomber: The Story of the Berlin Airlift's "Chocolate Pilot,"* Michael O'Tunnell

IDEAS FOR TALKING ABOUT EVENTS OF THE PAST:

Search together online for information about other people who have faced the challenges of a hostile environment and responded with heroic action that positively impacted others:

- *What happened?*
- *How does this person build our knowledge of heroism?*

CREDITS

Great Minds® has made every effort to obtain permission for the reprinting of all copyrighted material. If any owner of copyrighted material is not acknowledged herein, please contact Great Minds® for proper acknowledgment in all future editions and reprints of this module.

- All material from the *Common Core State Standards for English Language Arts & Literacy in History/Social Studies, Science, and Technical Subjects* © Copyright 2010 National Governors Association Center for Best Practices and Council of Chief State School Officers. All rights reserved.
- Handout 13A: "Century-Old Lessons from the 'Bottom of the World'" by William Sisson from Soundings magazine, April 2013. Copyrighted 2016. Active Interest Media. 126874:1216SH
- Handout 28B: "Malala Yousafzai – Nobel Lecture" by Malala Yousafzai, Oslo, 10 December 2014. Copyright © The Nobel Foundation (2014) Source: http://nobelprize.org
- All images are used under license from Shutterstock.com unless otherwise noted.
- For updated credit information, please visit **http://witeng.link/credits**.

ACKNOWLEDGMENTS

Great Minds® Staff

The following writers, editors, reviewers, and support staff contributed to the development of this curriculum.

Ann Brigham, Lauren Chapalee, Sara Clarke, Emily Climer, Lorraine Griffith, Emily Gula, Sarah Henchey, Trish Huerster, Stephanie Kane-Mainier, Lior Klirs, Liz Manolis, Andrea Minich, Lynne Munson, Marya Myers, Rachel Rooney, Aaron Schifrin, Danielle Shylit, Rachel Stack, Sarah Turnage, Michelle Warner, Amy Wierzbicki, Margaret Wilson, and Sarah Woodard.

Colleagues and Contributors

We are grateful for the many educators, writers, and subject-matter experts who made this program possible.

David Abel, Robin Agurkis, Elizabeth Bailey, Julianne Barto, Amy Benjamin, Andrew Biemiller, Charlotte Boucher, Sheila Byrd-Carmichael, Eric Carey, Jessica Carloni, Janine Cody, Rebecca Cohen, Elaine Collins, Tequila Cornelious, Beverly Davis, Matt Davis, Thomas Easterling, Jeanette Edelstein, Kristy Ellis, Moira Clarkin Evans, Charles Fischer, Marty Gephart, Kath Gibbs, Natalie Goldstein, Christina Gonzalez, Mamie Goodson, Nora Graham, Lindsay Griffith, Brenna Haffner, Joanna Hawkins, Elizabeth Haydel, Steve Hettleman, Cara Hoppe, Ashley Hymel, Carol Jago, Jennifer Johnson, Mason Judy, Gail Kearns, Shelly Knupp, Sarah Kushner, Shannon Last, Suzanne Lauchaire, Diana Leddy, David Liben, Farren Liben, Jennifer Marin, Susannah Maynard, Cathy McGath, Emily McKean, Jane Miller, Rebecca Moore, Cathy Newton, Turi Nilsson, Julie Norris, Galemarie Ola, Michelle Palmieri, Meredith Phillips, Shilpa Raman, Tonya Romayne, Emmet Rosenfeld, Jennifer Ruppel, Mike Russoniello, Deborah Samley, Casey Schultz, Renee Simpson, Rebecca Sklepovich, Amelia Swabb, Kim Taylor, Vicki Taylor, Melissa Thomson Lindsay Tomlinson, Melissa Vail, Keenan Walsh, Julia Wasson, Lynn Welch, Yvonne Guerrero Welch, Emily Whyte, Lynn Woods, and Rachel Zindler.

Early Adopters

The following early adopters provided invaluable insight and guidance for Wit & Wisdom:

- Bourbonnais School District 53 • Bourbonnais, IL
- Coney Island Prep Middle School • Brooklyn, NY
- Gate City Charter School for the Arts • Merrimack, NH
- Hebrew Academy for Special Children • Brooklyn, NY
- Paris Independent Schools • Paris, KY
- Saydel Community School District • Saydel, IA
- Strive Collegiate Academy • Nashville, TN
- Valiente College Preparatory Charter School • South Gate, CA
- Voyageur Academy • Detroit, MI

Design Direction provided by Alton Creative, Inc.

Project management support, production design, and copyediting services provided by **ScribeConcepts.com**

Copyediting services provided by Fine Lines Editing

Product management support provided by Sandhill Consulting